RECEIVED

D0482338

R)

GREAT HISPANIC AND LATINO AMERICANS

Cesar Chavez

by Christine Juarez

CAPSTONE PRESS
a capstone imprint

Pebble Books are published by Capstone Press,
1710 Roe Crest Drive, North Mankato, Minnesota 56003
www.mycapstone.com

Library of Congress Cataloging-in-Publication Data
Names: Juarez, Christine, 1976–
Title: Cesar Chavez / by Christine Juarez.
Description: North Mankato, Minnesota : Capstone Press, 2017. | Series: Pebble
books. Great Hispanic and Latino Americans | Audience: K to grade 3. | Includes
bibliographical references and index.
Identifiers: LCCN 2016003677 | ISBN 9781515718925 (library binding) |
ISBN 9781515719038 (paperback) | ISBN 9781515719236 (eBook pdf)
Subjects: LCSH: Chavez, Cesar, 1927–1993—Juvenile literature. |
Labor leaders—United States—Biography—Juvenile literature. | Mexican
Americans—Biography—Juvenile literature. | Mexican American migrant
agricultural laborers—Biography—Juvenile literature. | United Farm Workers—
History—Juvenile literature. | Migrant agricultural laborers—Labor unions—
United States—History—Juvenile literature.
Classification: LCC HD6509.C48 J83 2017 | DDC 331.88/13092—dc23
LC record available at http://lccn.loc.gov/2016003677

Note to Parents and Teachers

The Great Hispanic and Latino Americans series supports national
curriculum standards for social studies related to people, places,
and culture. This book describes and illustrates Cesar Chavez.
The images support early readers in understanding the text. The
repetition of words and phrases helps early readers learn new
words. This book also introduces early readers to subject-specific
vocabulary words, which are defined in the Glossary section. Early
readers may need assistance to read some words and to use the
Table of Contents, Glossary, Read More, Internet Sites, and Index
sections of the book.

Printed in the United States of America in North Mankato, Minnesota.
009663F16

Table of Contents

1927
born

Early Years

Cesar Chavez was a leader and an organizer. He worked for the rights of farmworkers. He helped workers get paid and treated fairly. Cesar was born March 31, 1927.

Cesar's parents, Librado and Juana, in the 1970s

1927
born

Cesar's parents were from Mexico. They moved to Arizona before Cesar was born. His parents taught Cesar and his brothers and sisters to be kind to all people.

a family picking onions

1927
born

1938
family sells farm
and moves to
California

Young Cesar went to school and worked on his family's farm. In 1938 Cesar's family sold their farm and moved to California. There, the family went from farm to farm picking crops.

workers harvesting a crop

1927
born

1938
family sells farm
and moves to
California

Cesar and his family were migrant workers. Life was hard for them. Farm owners paid workers very little. Workers often were not paid what they were owed. Picking crops was hot, tiring work. Some owners made workers pay for drinking water.

An owner (right) looks on as workers pack celery.

1927
born

1938
family sells farm
and moves to
California

12

Cesar's father taught his family
to strike over poor treatment.
They would stop working
in the fields and leave.
Cesar's father did not want
them to work for an owner
who treated workers badly.

Cesar and his wife, Helen, in the 1970s

1927	1938	1944	1948
born	family sells farm and moves to California	joins U.S. Navy	marries Helen Fabela

Starting a Union

In 1944 Cesar joined the U.S. Navy.

Then in 1948 he married Helen Fabela.

They had eight children.

Back in California, Cesar returned

to picking crops. He listened to

the workers. He heard their stories

of poor treatment.

1927	1938	1944	1948
born	family sells farm and moves to California	joins U.S. Navy	marries Helen Fabela

Cesar wanted to help all farmworkers. In 1952 Cesar took a job teaching workers about their rights. In 1962 Cesar started a union. Together farmworkers would demand fair pay and treatment.

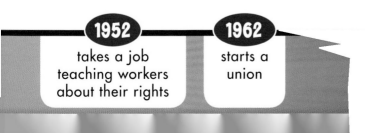

1952 takes a job teaching workers about their rights

1962 starts a union

1927
born

1938
family sells farm
and moves to
California

1944
joins
U.S.
Navy

1948
marries
Helen
Fabela

Cesar led the union in a five-year strike against grape farm owners. Both the owners and the workers were angry. Cesar stopped eating for a time. He wanted his fasting to remind both sides to be peaceful.

1952
takes a job teaching workers about their rights

1962
starts a union

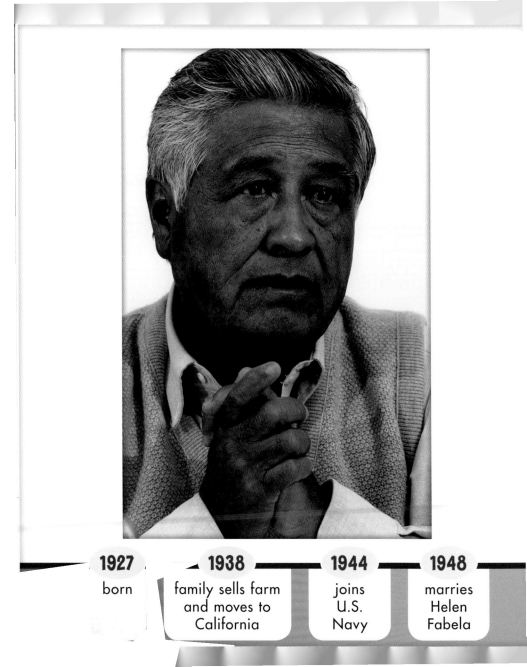

1927	1938	1944	1948
born	family sells farm and moves to California	joins U.S. Navy	marries Helen Fabela

Remembering Cesar

Cesar spent his life standing up for farmworkers. He used strikes and fasts to bring about change peacefully. Cesar died April 23, 1993. He is remembered every March 31 on Cesar Chavez Day.

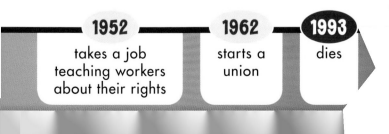

1952 takes a job teaching workers about their rights

1962 starts a union

1993 dies

Glossary

demand—to strongly ask for or request something

fast—to go without food for a certain length of time

migrant worker—a worker who moves from farm to farm

right—something one can or must do by law

strike—when a group of workers stops doing their job to try to force the person in charge to treat them better

union—a group of workers that tries to gain more rights, such as fair pay and safer jobs

Read More

Brown, Moncia. *Side by Side: The Story of Dolores Huerta and Cesar Chavez.* New York: Rayo, 2010.

Gregory, Josh. *Cesar Chavez.* A True Book. New York: Children's Press, 2015.

Internet Sites

FactHound offers a safe, fun way to find Internet sites related to this book. All of the sites on FactHound have been researched by our staff.

Here's all you do:

Visit *www.facthound.com*

Type in this code: 9781515718925

 Check out projects, games and lots more at
www.capstonekids.com

Index

Editorial Credits
Erika L. Shores, editor; Charmaine Whitman, designer;
Kelly Garvin, media researcher; Tori Abraham, production specialist

Photo Credits
Corbis/Farrell Grehan, 16; Getty Images: American Stock Archive, 12, Arthur Schatz/
The LIFE Picture Collection, cover, 1, 18, Buyenlarge, 10, Cathy Murphy, 6, 14, Geoff
Hansen, 20, John W. Keith/Hulton Archive, 8, Tim Graham/Evening Standard, 4
Artistic Elements: Shutterstock: Eliks, nalinn, tuulijumala